SandCastle™
Animal Groups

A Zeal
of Zebras

ANIMAL GROUPS
ON AN AFRICAN SAFARI

Alex Kuskowski

CONSULTING EDITOR, DIANE CRAIG, M.A./READING SPECIALIST

ABDO
Publishing Company

visit us at www.abdopublishing.com

Published by ABDO Publishing Company, a division of ABDO, P.O. Box 398166, Minneapolis, Minnesota 55439. Copyright © 2013 by Abdo Consulting Group, Inc. International copyrights reserved in all countries. No part of this book may be reproduced in any form without written permission from the publisher. SandCastle™ is a trademark and logo of ABDO Publishing Company.

Printed in the United States of America, North Mankato, Minnesota
062012
092012

 PRINTED ON RECYCLED PAPER

Editor: Liz Salzmann
Content Developer: Nancy Tuminelly
Cover and Interior Design and Production: Anders Hanson, Mighty Media, Inc.
Photo Credits: Shutterstock

Library of Congress Cataloging-in-Publication Data
Kuskowski, Alex.
  A zeal of zebras : animal groups on an African safari / Alex Kuskowski.
     p. cm. -- (Animal groups)
  ISBN 978-1-61783-543-8
  1. Savanna animals--Behavior--Africa--Juvenile literature. 2. Social behavior in animals--Africa--Juvenile literature. I. Title.
  QL336.K87 2013
  591.7´48--dc23
                        2012009608

SANDCASTLE™ LEVEL: FLUENT

SandCastle™ books are created by a team of professional educators, reading specialists, and content developers around five essential components—phonemic awareness, phonics, vocabulary, text comprehension, and fluency—to assist young readers as they develop reading skills and strategies and increase their general knowledge. All books are written, reviewed, and leveled for guided reading, early reading intervention, and Accelerated Reader® programs for use in shared, guided, and independent reading and writing activities to support a balanced approach to literacy instruction. The SandCastle™ series has four levels that correspond to early literacy development. The levels are provided to help teachers and parents select appropriate books for young readers.

Emerging Readers
(no flags)

Beginning Readers
(1 flag)

Transitional Readers
(2 flags)

Fluent Readers
(3 flags)

Contents

African Safari Animals

Many animals live in Africa. It has a lot of **savannas** and rivers. The animals wander many miles. They spend time looking for food and water.

Why Live in a Group?

Animals often live in groups. Animals in a group can **protect** each other. They can share space, food, and water. They also work together to help raise babies. Many animal groups have fun names!

A Zeal of Zebras

A zeal of zebras **confuses** predators. Each zebra has a different set of stripes. In a group, the stripes **blend** together.

Zebra Names

MALE
stallion

FEMALE
mare

BABY
colt, foal

GROUP
zeal, herd

A Coalition of Cheetahs

Cheetahs in a group are called a coalition. They use their good eyesight to spot **prey**. They hunt together to catch it.

Cheetah Names

MALE	**BABY**
male	*cub*
FEMALE	**GROUP**
female	*coalition*

A Stand of Flamingos

A group of flamingos is called a stand. Some stands have thousands of flamingos. They eat a lot of **algae** and **shrimp** every day. It turns them pink.

Flamingo Names

MALE
cock

BABY
chick

FEMALE
hen

GROUP
stand

A Mob of Meerkats

Meerkat mobs live in **burrows**. They **forage** for food during the day. They stay in their burrows at night.

Meerkat Names

MALE	**BABY**
male	*pup*
FEMALE	**GROUP**
female	*mob, gang*

A Parade of Elephants

Elephants live in groups called parades. They are very **affectionate**. They hug by wrapping their **trunks** together.

Elephant Names

MALE
bull

BABY
calf

FEMALE
cow

GROUP
parade, herd

A Journey of Giraffes

A group of giraffes is called a journey. Giraffes watch out for each other. An adult giraffe looks after baby giraffes while the others eat.

Giraffe Names

MALE
bull

FEMALE
doe

BABY
calf

GROUP
journey, corps, tower, group

A Bloat of Hippos

A group of hippos is called a bloat. Hippos spend most of the day in the water. At night they go on land to eat grass.

Hippo Names

MALE
bull

FEMALE
cow

BABY
calf

GROUP
bloat, herd

More

AFRICAN SAFARI GROUPS

A herd of
antelope

A pride
of lions

A congress
of baboons

A nest
of vipers

A gang
of buffalo

A flock
of camels

A clan
of hyenas

A crash
of rhinos

Quiz

1. Zebra stripes **blend** together in a group. *True or false?*

2. Cheetahs have bad eyesight. *True or false?*

3. Flamingos eat food that makes them pink. *True or false?*

4. Elephants are not **affectionate**. *True or false?*

5. Hippos go on land at night. *True or false?*

Glossary

affectionate – loving and tender.

algae – a water plant such as seaweed.

blend – to match so that you can't tell one from another.

burrow – a hole or tunnel dug in the ground by a small animal for use as shelter.

confuse – to make uncertain or unclear.

forage – to search for food.

prey – an animal that is hunted or caught for food.

protect – to guard someone or something from harm or danger.

savanna – a large area of land covered with grasses.

shrimp – a small shellfish often caught for food.

trunk – an elephant's upper lip and long nose.